D0049577

A Keepsake Book from the
Heart of the Home

LOVE

by

Susan Branch

MY BOOK Donna Pelzman

Little, Brown & Company
Boston   Toronto   London
New York

FIRST EDITION
ISBN 0-316-10658-5

♥ Excerpt from "Moonlight Becomes You" by Johnny Burke & Jimmy Van Heusen. Copyright 1942 by Famous Music Corporation, © renewed 1970 by Famous Music Corporation. Used by permission.

♥ "The Rose" by Amanda McBroom. © 1977 Warner-Tamerlane Publishing Corp. & Third Story Music Inc. All Rights Reserved. Used by permission.

♥ Dedication page quote by Lowman Pauling & Ralph Bass.

Published simultaneously in Canada by Little, Brown & Company (Canada) Limited

PRINTED IN SINGAPORE

TELL ALL THE STARS ABOVE. THIS IS DEDICATED TO THE ONE I LOVE.

For J BH

"Beautiful faces are
those that wear
Whole-souled honesty
printed there."

Ellen Palmer Allerton

PRESENTING

FOR YOUR PERUSAL

La Table de la Contents

. . . and much,
much,
more.

WHAT IS LOVE?

LOVE IS LOVE'S REWARD. John Dryden ♥ LOVE IS NOT TO BE TRIFLED WITH. French Proverb ♥ LOVE IS A MANY SPLENDORED THING. Paul Francis Webster LOVE MAKES THE WORLD GO ROUND. French Song ♥ LOVE DOESN'T MAKE THE WORLD GO ROUND. LOVE IS WHAT MAKES THE RIDE WORTHWHILE. Franklin P. Jones ♥ LOVE KNOWS NO BOUNDS. Anonymous ♥ WHAT IS LOVE? FIVE FEET OF HEAVEN IN A PONYTAIL! Morton & Michaels ♥ LOVE IS BLIND. Chaucer ♥ LOVE IS THE ONLY GAME THAT IS NOT CALLED ON ACCOUNT OF DARKNESS. Anonymous ♥ LOVE IS HEAVEN AND HEAVEN IS LOVE. Sir Walter Scott ♥ LOVE IS THE TRIUMPH OF IMAGINATION OVER INTELLIGENCE. H.L. Mencken ♥ LOVE IS ALL YOU NEED. The Beatles ♥ LOVE IS THE THING. Anonymous WHAT IS LOVE?...

$\mathcal{L}$OVE IS THE
IRRESISTIBLE DESIRE
TO BE DESIRED
IRRESISTIBLY.
♡ Louis Ginsberg

OWN YOURSELF

THINK IT OVER

TAKE YOUR TIME

BE SURE

LOOK BEFORE YOU LEAP

TO THINE OWNSELF BE TRUE

FOREVER IS A LONG,

LONG TIME...

ADVICE TO WOMEN

"The art of flirtation is dying. A man & woman are either in love these days or just friends. In the realm of love, reticence & sophistication go hand in hand, for one of the joys of life is discovery." ♥ Marya Mannes

8

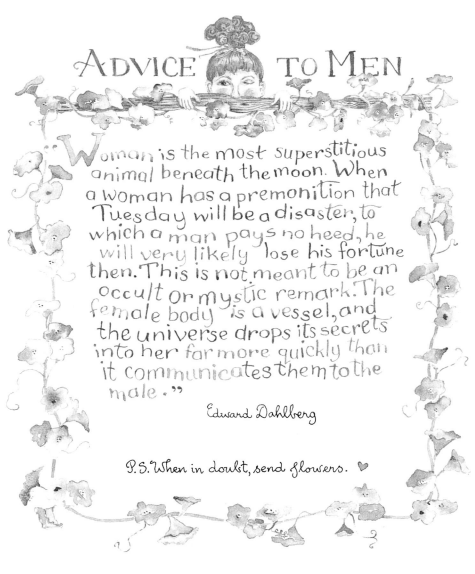

ADVICE TO MEN

Woman is the most superstitious animal beneath the moon. When a woman has a premonition that Tuesday will be a disaster, to which a man pays no heed, he will very likely lose his fortune then. This is not meant to be an occult or mystic remark. The female body is a vessel, and the universe drops its secrets into her far more quickly than it communicates them to the male."

Edward Dahlberg

P.S. When in doubt, send flowers. ♡

9

SPEAKING of FLOWERS

In the 1700s it was common to communicate through flowers ~ apparently they had nothing to do all day but to spend their time figuring out these love knots ~ a pastime full of charm. ♥ Here are a few common flowers & their meanings for those of you in a hurry ~ but still feeling charming. ♥♥

First & foremost are Roses ~ all roses mean love, dedicated to the Goddess of Love ~ cabbage roses are Ambassadors of Love while rosebuds mean Young Love. ♥

A bouquet of red **Tulips** is an Overt Declaration of Love.

Peach Blossoms say "I belong to you."

Give Lilacs or Lavender to your New Love.

When you send Heartsease you say "Think of Me."

Lemon Blossoms promise "I'll be True to You."

For Happiness Anew, a bouquet of Lily of the Valley

Keep a Forget-me-not in your locket for True Love.

Flower  Lingo

SWEET PEAS

A bunch of fragrant Sweet Peas says Bon Voyage.

Ranunculus mean "You Sparkle with Charm."

For Fertility the symbol is the Marigold

Honeysuckle means Sweet Natured.

"Thinking of You" says the Zinnia

Columbine would question the Sanity of the Receiver as in "Are you Nuts?"

For the final straw, send Tansy to say "This Means War."

"Some flowers spoke with strong and powerful voices, which proclaimed in accents trumpet-tongued, 'I am beautiful, and I rule.' Others murmured in tones scarcely audible, but exquisitely soft and sweet, ' I am little, and I am beloved.' "

♥ George Sand

ROSES ARE RED

VIOLETS ARE BLUE

SUGAR IS SWEET

AND SO ARE YOU

"IT WAS ROSES, ROSES, ALL THE WAY
WITH MYRTLE MIXED IN MY PATH LIKE MAD."
ROBT. BROWNING

I remember wearing a gardenia corsage — my first — to a party years ago. All night the fragrance of that old-fashioned flower seemed to weave a spell reminding me of how special an evening it was.

Mark Twain (darling man) said, "Whatever a man's age, he can reduce it several years by putting a bright-colored flower in his buttonhole."

T here you have it — two testimonials on the charm & power of the flower. We (me 'n Mark) suggest you send a boutonniere or corsage to loved ones every chance you get: first day of spring, Mother's Day, a new job, Christmas, Midsummer's Eve, graduation, May Day, start of a great vacation, or just because. ♥

Valentine Toasts

She says

Here's to one and only one
And may that one be he,
Who loves but one and only one,
And may that one be me.

anon.

He says

Give me a kisse, and to that kisse a score;
Then to that twenty, adde a hundred more;
A thousand to that hundred; so kiss on,
To make that thousand up a million;
Treble that million, and when that is done
Let's kisse afresh, as when we first begun.

Robt. Herrick

They say

Here's to you both
a beautiful pair,
we celebrate
your love affair.

Dinner For Two

MENU

Cabernet Sauvignon
Caesar Salad
Steak au Poivre
Potatoes Anna
Strawberry Shortcake

"Across the gateway of my heart
I wrote 'No Thoroughfare'
But love came laughing by, and cried:
'I enter everywhere.'"
Herbert Shipman

15

STEAK AU POIVRE

Serves Two

1–1½ tbsp. cracked black pepper
2 tenderloin steaks – 1¼" thick
2 tbsp. butter
1 tbsp. shallots, minced

2 tbsp. cognac
2 tbsp. red wine
¼ c. beef broth
2 tbsp. heavy cream

Press the pepper into the raw steaks. Heat the butter in a heavy skillet. Sear steaks over med.~high heat, both sides, turning with tongs. Reduce heat to med. & cook until desired doneness. Remove steaks from pan & keep warm. Add shallots to pan & sauté a minute or so. Add cognac & wine — boil 2 min., stirring. Add beef broth, boil 2 more min., scraping up bits from pan. Stir in cream, heat but don't boil. Pour sauce over steaks & serve. ♥

Tonight.
Same time.
Same place.

POTATOES ANNA

♥ Serves Two ♥

This is the kind of recipe that inspires life-long devotion — he'll/she'll never let you go!

3 large Idaho potatoes
1/4 c. butter, melted
salt & freshly ground pepper
sour cream & fresh chives (opt.)

Preheat oven to 425°. Peel potatoes & carefully slice them into 1/16" rounds. Put about 1 Tbsp. butter into a small oven-proof skillet. Thoroughly dry each slice of potato with paper towels as you line the bottom of the pan with overlapping slices. Dribble or brush on a bit more butter, salt & pepper & continue layering in this way until potatoes are used up. Bake 50 min. & press potatoes down with spatula every so often. Turn heat up to 500° & cook another 10 min. Turn out onto a plate & serve with sour cream & chives.

"'Stay' is a charming word in a friend's vocabulary."
Louisa May Alcott

Signs of Love

See the book <u>Love</u> <u>Signs</u> by Linda Goodman
for complete information astrologically speaking. ♥

Your Sun Sign	Best Match	Element
Aries	Sagittarius & Leo	Fire
Taurus	Virgo & Capricorn	Earth
Gemini	Libra & Aquarius	Air
Cancer	Scorpio & Pisces	Water
Leo.	Aries & Sagittarius	Fire
Virgo	Taurus & Capricorn	Earth
Libra	Gemini & Aquarius	Air
Scorpio	Cancer & Pisces	Water
Sagittarius	Aries & Leo	Fire
Capricorn	Taurus & Virgo	Earth
Aquarius	Gemini & Libra	Air
Pisces	Cancer & Scorpio	Water

Most often you will find an easy harmony & understanding
with those in your own element — Fire with Fire, etc.
This of course is not written in stone ♥ (it's in the stars).

" Love in its essence is spiritual fire. "

Emanuel Swedenborg

Red & White Roses

Unity

Sure shot

LOVE POTION

Secretly put 3 drops of Tincture of Rose in something your intended ~~victim~~ oops! lover is about to drink. To make the tincture, the potion, the Powerful Elixir of Love, mix together 25 white rose petals, 25 red rose petals & 50 forget-me-nots in a saucepan. With a dropper add 365 drops of water taken from a free-flowing body of fresh water. Bring to a boil. Strain before serving. Strongest when petals & flowers are gathered at first light.

Forget-me-not

True Love

Cheers!

Skoal!

Bottoms up!

"The kiss originated when the first male reptile licked the first female reptile, implying in a subtle, complimentary way that she was as succulent as the small reptile he had for dinner the night before."
♥ F. Scott Fitzgerald

"MA CHÉRIE —
SANS VOUS JE NE SUIS
QU'UN VER DE TERRE"

FRENCH STUFF

I remember specifically the first time I heard of French kissing. I was in the 7th grade, walking across the gym field toward home with my best friend who had found out about it that day & was eager to pass on her information. I was totally taken aback ~ I really couldn't believe my ears! (I had already touched tongues with my little brother years before & had found it yukky, to put it mildly.) As far as I was concerned we had just entered the realm of never~never land. No creepy French kissing, thank you anyway. ♥

Ahhh, the French. French doors, French bread, French toast, French fries — how could I question!? And now for the language of love~here are a few French phrases ~ if the accent & the moment are right it almost doesn't matter what they mean:

Vous êtes un ange.
You are an angel.

Sans vous je ne suis qu'un ver de terre.
I am only an earthworm without you.

Que vous fait rêver?
What makes you dream?

Cela m'est bien égal que le soleil ne se lève plus, si seulement vous m'aimez.
I don't care if the sun never rises again as long as you love me.

Vous êtes une super nana.
You are one fabulous babe.

Ma tourterelle   Mon chou   Mon amour   Mon minet
My dove   My cabbage   My love   My kitten   ♥ ♥

FOOD & LOVE

I remember my very first chocolate eclair. I was about 5 years old & I was spending the day with my grandma. We were all dressed up & she took me downtown to a big department store that smelled like perfume. She bought me a pair of red leather shoes with a strap across the top & three little teardrop cutouts over the toe. I thought nothing could be better than this but afterwards she took me into a cake & pastry-filled bakery where everything seemed to be covered in whipped cream & chocolate. We sat in a booth in the window & my eclair was served on a plate with its own lace doily. The tender biscuit, filled with rich cream & covered in chocolate, melted in my mouth. I never tasted anything like it — it was wonderful, so, so delicious — I think I saw stars. I looked with new respect & wonder at my grandma, keeper of the keys, mystery woman, knower of all things fantastic.

All Chocolate

Menu

Aphrodisiac City

Chocolate Truffles
Chocolate Mousse
Chocolate Eclairs
Death by Chocolate

"There's nothing half so sweet in life as love's young dream."

Clement C. Moore

Truffles

A wonderful gift for Christmas or Valentine's Day,
truffles are quick & easy to make. Make your after-
dinner coffee more special by serving these melt-in-
your-mouth chocolate morsels alongside. ♥

6 oz. semi-sweet chocolate
2 egg yolks
2/3 c. unsalted butter, softened
1 1/3 c. powdered sugar, sifted
2 tsp. vanilla
1/2 c. walnuts, chopped
unsweetened cocoa powder
2 tsp. crème de menthe or Grand Marnier (opt.)

Over very low heat, slowly melt chocolate in a small
saucepan, stirring often. Remove from heat & cool.
Cream egg yolks & butter together. Add sugar slowly
& blend well. Pour the cooled chocolate into sugar
mixture; add vanilla & nuts. Stir. (If using a liqueur,
omit vanilla & substitute liqueur.) Refrigerate until
firm enough to handle. Shape into 1" balls; roll
in cocoa; chill. Keep refrigerated till ready to
serve. Can be frozen. ♥

CHOCOLATE MOUSSE

Serves Eight

8-oz. semisweet chocolate
¼ c. dark rum
½ c. sugar

2-3 Tbsp. lukewarm water
2 egg whites
2 c. heavy cream

Melt chocolate in top of double boiler. Meanwhile cook rum & sugar over very low heat till sugar melts (do not let it brown). Add sugar syrup to chocolate (they should be about the same temp.). Beat in 2 Tbsp. lukewarm water; set aside. Beat egg whites till stiff; whip cream & fold together. Beat chocolate again — if it has thickened, add 1 more Tbsp. water. Fold chocolate into cream & spoon into individual serving dishes or wine glasses. Chill.

Chocolate Eclairs

375° Makes 16 puffs

I shape my Chocolate Eclairs into little puffs ~ almost bite-sized. For a charming Valentines gift, line a pretty box with large paper doilies & fill the box with the puffs, each on its own small doily.

¼ c. butter ♥ ½ c. water ♥ ½ c. flour
2 eggs, room temp. ♥ 1½ c. heavy cream

Preheat oven to 375°. Boil butter & water together. Remove from heat & add flour all at once, beating rapidly till dough forms a ball. Cool 5 min. Add eggs one at a time, beating hard till dough is smooth. Butter & flour cookie sheets & drop dough by small teaspoonfuls 2" apart & bake 16 min. till brown & puffed. Put a little slit in each one; turn off the oven & put them back in 10 min. more. Cool. Whip cream with a little sugar & vanilla to taste. Cut off tops of puffs, fill with whipped cream, replace tops & spoon chocolate over.

Chocolate Sauce

Over low flame, heat 3 oz. semisweet chocolate & 2 Tbsp. butter, stirring. The sauce will thicken as it cools, so work quickly as you frost puffs. Refrigerate puffs.

"It is overdoing the thing to die of love."
♥ French Proverb

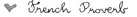

DEATH BY CHOCOLATE

350° Serves Eight

What a way to go. ♥ Your victim will love you. ♥ A chocolaty ice cream
cake roll finished off with a dollop of thick fudgy killer chocolate sauce. ♥

¼ c. cocoa	1 tsp. vanilla
1¼ c. powdered sugar	¼ tsp. salt
5 eggs	1 qt. good vanilla ice cream

Preheat oven to 350°. Sift cocoa & sugar together. Separate the eggs; put
the yolks & vanilla in a large bowl & beat very well until thick. In
another bowl whisk the egg whites till foamy; add salt & continue
beating till soft peaks are formed. Fold the cocoa & sugar into the whites,
then gently fold ⅓ of egg white mixture into the beaten yolks. Thoroughly butter a 10"×15" cookie sheet & line it with wax paper. Spread the
batter evenly in the pan; bake 18-20 min., until knife comes out clean.
Sprinkle a clean tea towel with powdered sugar & turn cake out onto it.
Remove wax paper & trim off any crispy edges. Roll the cake in the towel
from the long end ⬛↑ & let it rest 1-2 min. Unroll & let it rest again for a
few min., then roll it up again & allow it to cool completely. Set ice cream out to
soften. Unroll the cooled cake; spread evenly with ice cream & roll it back
up (without the tea towel). Dust the top with powdered sugar. Keep it in
the freezer till ready to serve. When ready, cut the cake & serve it with the
hot chocolate sauce on the side. ♥

Killer Chocolate Sauce

3 Tbsp. unsalted butter	1½ c. sugar
4 oz. unsweetened chocolate	7 Tbsp. corn syrup
⅔ c. boiling water	1 tsp. vanilla

Melt the butter & chocolate in a heavy saucepan over low heat; add boiling
water & stir well. Mix in the sugar & corn syrup ~ till sauce is smooth. Boil
the sauce, without stirring, for 10 min.; remove from heat; cool 20 min., then
add the vanilla. Spoon the sauce over the ice cream cake and serve. ♥

Give me my Romeo; and when
 he shall die,
Take him and cut him out in little
 stars,
And he will make the face of
 heaven so fine
That all the world will be in
 love with night
And pay no worship to the
 garish sun.

William Shakespeare

APHRODISIACS

"THY BATHS SHALL BE THE JUICE OF JULY-FLOWERS, SPIRIT OF ROSES, AND OF VIOLETS." Ben Jonson

FRESH RIPE PEACHES, BUTTERMILK BATHS, APRICOT BRANDY, GOOSE FAT, POWDERED UNICORN HORN, CHERRIES & CHERRY JUICE.

"I want to do with you what spring does with the cherry trees."
Pablo Neruda

GAZING AT SWANS; FROGS LEGS, FLOWERS & FIGS; THE SERENADE & LOVE SONG; BEGUILING SILK PAJAMAS; ONIONS, OYSTERS, ANCHOVIES & POMEGRANATES.

THE GREEK BIOGRAPHER PLUTARCH WROTE THAT THE BODY OF ALEXANDER THE GREAT GAVE OFF THE SCENT OF VIOLETS.

Yum...

PERFUME, DANCING, LOBSTERS, CHAMPAGNE, CINNAMON, TRUFFLES, HOT MARSHMALLOWS (TOASTED OVER AN OPEN FIRE), BASIL, PINENUTS, GINSENG, CAVIAR, & FATTED SUCKLING PIGS.

Romance is a celebration of the senses — a celebration of being Alive. Here are some ideas:

Go through revolving doors with both of you in the same slot. Go into phone booths together. 💙

Saturday night, 6-8 p.m. with Garrison Keillor on public radio — a lovely evening. 💜

Hide little surprises in suitcases, under the pillow, in the medicine cabinet — a note, candy, a funny comic strip. 💜

Brides magazines are a great place to look for romantic vacation ideas. 💜

A limo is a wonderful luxury — hire one for a trip to the airport, to the train station, or even just out to a special dinner. 💜

Dedicate a song over the radio. 💜

Give butterfly kisses. Wash each other's hair. Lie in the grass & watch the stars. 💜

SPREAD SUNSHINE

Does he love coffee? Get him a 50 lb. box of his favorite kind. Are Nutty Buddies her cup of tea? Fill the freezer. Do it up BIG! ♥

Get dressed up on Sundays. Go visiting, stop in on your friends, take food. ♥

If one of you has to go away, a good gift is stationery and lots of LOVE stamps. You can seal His letters with a kiss (use lots of lipstick). ♥

I've always made my own B'day banners but not anymore. Now I call 800-322-6637 & order their giant banners — 10' to 30' long, a foot high & you can say anything — "I love you my darling angel from heaven" or "Hey Joe! Look in the car!" Good for Anniversaries, Valentine's Day, Marriage, Proposals ♥

Godiva Chocolates — the only way to fly. They also have boxes of pink or blue-banded cigars for new daddies. 800-643-1579. ♥

"Imagination is more important than knowledge."
♥ Albert Einstein

ICE BREAKER

Feeling shy? This is a flirtatious little game that gets people talking; by the time you're done, you'll be old friends. You need a little piece of paper — I learned it on a cocktail napkin. ♥

The party of the first part (that's you) should ask the party of the second part to write down the answers to these questions:

1. What is your favorite animal? Why?
2. If you were an animal what would you be & why?
3. What's your favorite kind of weather? Why?
4. Name your favorite body of water (lake, river, waterfall, lagoon, etc.). Why?

The party of the second part now repeats his answers to you as you magically, competently & cutely interpret:

#1. is how you see yourself.
2. is how others see you.
3. shows your romantic nature.
4. **describes** your feelings about sex.

The heart speaks in many ways.

D R E A M S

CAN FORETELL THE FUTURE

DREAMS OF FLOWERS=

GREAT PROSPERITY

OF A FAMILY WIZARD= RICHES

OF A TAME WOLF=

WILL BE KISSED OFTEN

OF HAVING
NICE ELBOWS=
GOOD TIMES
ARE
COMING

OF EATING
CAULIFLOWER=
JOY & HONOR

OF EATING EGGS=

=AN EARLY MARRIAGE

OF AN ANGRY CAT=

OF WATER=
A
B
U
N
D
A
N
C
E

WILL ARGUE WITH
LOVER

OF PLUMS

A SECRET LOVE

By the light of the
silvery moon,...
We'll croon love's tune~

SEAL IT WITH   A KISS ♥

"Some fall in love with women who are rich, aristocratic or stupid. I am attracted by those who mysteriously hold out a promise of the integrity which I have lost: unsubdued daughters of Isis, beautiful as night, tumultuous as the moon-stirred Atlantic."

♥ Cyril Connolly

Wild Thing,
    You make my
heart sing—
    You make everything
groovy. ♡   The Troggs

Hi! Guess w...   Febr...

ROMANTIC BREAKFAST

Have these heavenly sensual breakfasts in bed or on the lawn under a tree. Cultivate an attitude: romance is not about denial & diets & neither are these breakfast menus! Benjamin Franklin, intelligent moral man, said, "Take time for all things" — this includes *Bliss* ♥

German Pancake with
Powdered Sugar & Heated
Maple Syrup

Watermelon Balls

Thick-cut Bacon Strips

Baked Bananas
with Vanilla Ice Cream

Fresh Squeezed O.J.
mixed with Sparkling Water

German Pancake

Yum!   Four Servings

4 eggs
2/3 c. flour
1 tsp. salt
2/3 c. milk
3 Tbsp. butter

Butter a heavy 10" oven-proof skillet. Preheat oven to 450°. Beat the eggs with a whisk to blend. Slowly add flour; beat well. Stir in salt & milk. Pour batter into skillet & drop the butter by teaspoonfuls into the batter, spreading evenly. Bake at 450° for 15 min. — reduce heat to 350° & bake another 10 min. Remove from oven & sift powdered sugar over the top. Serve with heated maple syrup. ♥

Baked Bananas

Put one large ripe banana per person on a cookie sheet (in its skin). Bake in a preheated 350° oven for about 20 min. — till skins turn completely black. Slit open & moosh up, same as you would with a baked potato. Delicious when cuddled with a big scoop of vanilla ice cream & sprinkled with ground coffee beans.

Breakfast
MENU
♥

Heart-Shaped Waffles
Raspberry Syrup

Blueberries, Strawberries
& Raspberries

Sausage Links

One-half Cantaloupe with
a scoop of Vanilla
Ice Cream Inside

Hot Chocolate with Whipped
Cream & Red Zinger Iced Tea

A passionate 2-minute
kiss burns 50 calories!

Heart-Shaped
W A F F L E S

Serves 4-6

First you'll need a heart-shaped waffle iron, easy to find at a good kitchen-supply store.

2 eggs, beaten	1½ c. unbleached flour
1 c. + 2 Tbsp. milk	3 tsp. sugar
3 Tbsp. salad oil	3 tsp. baking powder

Follow instructions for your iron — oil & preheat. In a bowl with a pouring spout 🥛, beat eggs & whisk in milk & salad oil. Stir in dry ingredients ~ whisk to remove lumps. Pour into waffle iron & cook till very brown & crisp. Serve with heated raspberry syrup. 💜. Refrigerate any extra batter.

"Love is friendship set to music."

The Silver Screen

Old movies are so wonderful — here's a
short list of some of the most romantic
movies I've ever seen. Bring along a box of
tissues — prepare for a trip to the moon. ♡

Roman Holiday ~ Audrey Hepburn, Gregory Peck
The Apartment ~ Jack Lemmon, Shirley MacLaine
Sabrina ~ Wm. Holden, Audrey Hepburn, Humphrey Bogart
Splendor in the Grass ~ Natalie Wood, Warren Beatty
An Affair to Remember ~ Cary Grant, Deborah Kerr
Love with the Proper Stranger ~ Natalie Wood,
      Steve McQueen
A New Kind of Love ~ Joanne Woodward, Paul Newman
The More the Merrier ~ Joel McCrea, Jean Arthur
The World of Suzie Wong ~ Wm. Holden, Nancy Kwan
Love Among the Ruins ~ Katharine Hepburn,
      Laurence Olivier
A Stolen Life ~ Bette Davis, Glenn Ford
Enchanted Cottage ~ Robt. Young, Dorothy McGuire
Somewhere in Time ~ Christopher Reeve, Jane Seymour
Born Yesterday ~ Wm. Holden, Judy Holliday
The Ghost & Mrs Muir ~ Gene Tierney

FRED ASTAIRE AND GINGER ROGERS!

Despite our differences, men & women (& children too!) crave the same things: love, understanding, nurturing, respect, security & appreciation. You can almost always see the sweet eight-year-old in the face of any grown-up person. 🤍

KID STUFF
for big people

sing in THE CAR

Go Camping

Build Sand Castles

run, dance, play

play with yo-yos

Fly a Kite

Ride a Bicycle Built for Two

Play Post Office

JUGGLE   explore   the world

Climb into   a hammock together

PLAY "WHAT if   WE HAD A
MILLION DOLLARS"

eat Lik-m-aid, ice cream
cones & other forbidden food

lick bowl & beaters

DO STUFF WITH GUSTO

play doctor

"EVERYBODY LOVES A BABY THAT'S WHY
I'M IN LOVE WITH YOU." Pretty Baby

POTIONS, SPELLS, SUPERSTITIONS OF LOVE

PIN IVY TO YOUR BREAST ON NEW YEAR'S DAY – YOU WILL MARRY THE NEXT MAN/WOMAN YOU SPEAK TO. (DON'T JUST BE TALKING TO ANYBODY.) ♥

MAKE A TEA FROM HEARTSEASE. BRUSH COOL LIQUID OVER EYELIDS OF SLEEPING LOVED ONE. HE WILL LOVE THE FIRST ONE HE SEES. DRINK TEA TO CURE HEARTBREAK. ♥

BLOW ALL OF THE FEATHERY REMAINS OFF A BLOWN DANDELION FLOWER WITH ONE BREATH. YOU WILL GET YOUR WISH.

JUST BEFORE BED, HARD BOIL AN EGG, CUT IT IN HALF + DISCARD YOLK. SALT THE HALVES OF EGG. SIT ON SOMETHING YOU NEVER SAT ON BEFORE + EAT THE EGG. WALK TO BED BACKWARD. YOU WILL DREAM OF YOUR FUTURE MATE. ♥

TIE A NARROW BLUE SATIN RIBBON TO YOUR LEFT ANKLE – GO BARE-FOOT ALL DAY + YOU WILL SOON BE KISSED PROPERLY.

TO BE FOREVER BEAUTIFUL: AT EXACTLY SUNRISE ON THE FIRST OF MAY GO OUTSIDE AND ROLL NAKED IN THE DEW. ♥

IF YOU FIND A SMALL SPIDER IN THE FOLDS OF YOUR WEDDING DRESS YOU WILL NEVER BE POOR. ♥

FAIRY DUST

BAKE A WHOLE ALMOND INTO THE WEDDING CAKE + THE GUEST WHO FINDS IT WILL RECEIVE LONG LIFE AND PROSPERITY.

HOLD AN APPLE IN YOUR LEFT HAND, SAY "ADAM, ADAM, ADAM" 3 TIMES, BITE THE APPLE, HOLD YOUR BREATH, CHEW + SWALLOW. COMMUNICATION LINES ARE OPEN.

IF HE HAS BEEN UNFAITHFUL — TO GAIN YOU BACK HE MUST GATHER HAIR FROM THE FACE OF A WOLF (INCLUDING WHISKERS) – THEN BURN THEM + DRINK THE ASHES IN A SHOTGLASS FULL OF SOUR MILK. IF HE LIVES, YOU MAY FORGIVE HIM + BE CONFIDENT OF HIS FIDELITY. ♥

IF YOU CRY, CATCH YOUR TEARS IN A CUP, SPRINKLE THEM ON YOUR LOVER'S PILLOW – HE WILL EXPERI-ENCE A GREAT CHANGE OF HEART. ♥

AIR YOUR FEATHER QUILT ON A LINE THE FIRST CLEAR DAY AFTER THE VERNAL EQUINOX - PUT IT BACK ON THE BED – YOUR LOVE WILL BE REFRESHED AND RENEWED. ♥

THE STRAWBERRY
Nature's Valentine

We have
STRAWBERRY SHORTCAKE

And
STRAWBERRY CHEESECAKE

With
STRAWBERRY ICE CREAM

or
Chocolate~ dipped STRAWBERRIES

And
STRAWBERRY DAIQUIRIS

Don't forget the fat juicy garden variety straight off the bush & into the mouth. mmmm. ♥

DREAMS OF STRAWBERRIES ARE A GOOD OMEN.

STRAWBERRY SHORTCAKE

A delicious way to say I love you. ♥ Cream biscuits make the perfect delicate base for fresh berries. You'll need a heart-shaped cookie cutter, about 2 inches. ♥

To prepare strawberries & make them juicy: Keep back a few small, whole berries for garnish. Cut the rest in bite-sized pieces; sprinkle a couple of spoonfuls of sugar over & toss gently. Refrigerate for 1 hour.

BISCUITS

2 c. unbleached flour	2½ tsp. sugar
1 Tbsp. baking powder	1½ c. heavy cream
1 tsp. salt	4 Tbsp. melted butter

Preheat oven to 425°. With a fork, stir together flour, baking powder, salt & sugar. Slowly add 1 to 1½ c. cream, stirring constantly, just until dough comes together. Place dough on floured board & knead for 1 minute. Pat dough flat to about 3/4" thick. Cut with heart-shaped or round 2" cookie cutter & brush both sides with melted butter. Place them 1" apart on ungreased cookie sheet. Bake 15-18 min., till browned. (Makes about 14.)

To Serve   Whip cream with a spoon of sugar & a tsp. of vanilla, to taste. Split biscuits, spoon berries over bottom half — add a dollop of whipped cream, replace top ~ more berries & cream.

Strawberry Cheesecake
♥ chocolate crust ♥

Follow recipe on a box of Oreo Chocolate Cookie Crumbs for a 9" pie crust. ♥

♥ filling ♥

1 8 oz. pkg. cream cheese, softened   ½ tsp. vanilla
½ c. sugar   dash salt
1 Tbsp. lemon juice   2 eggs

Beat softened cream cheese till fluffy. Gradually blend in sugar, lemon juice, vanilla & salt. Add eggs, one at a time; beat well after each. Pour filling into crust. Bake at 325° for 25-30 min., till set.

♥ topping ♥

1½ c. sour cream   Combine all ingredients &
3 Tbsp. sugar   spoon over top of hot pie. Bake
¾ tsp. vanilla   10 min. more. Cool ~ chill well.

♥ strawberry glaze ♥

Cover top of pie with washed & stemmed, perfect, fresh strawberries, pointed end up. Slowly bring ½ c. clear red currant jelly or strawberry jelly (clear, no seeds) & 1 tsp. lemon juice to a slow boil, stirring. Spoon or brush glaze over berries — refrigerate. ♥

"You must always be awaggle with love."
D.H. Lawrence

49

STRAWBERRY ICE CREAM

I scream, you scream, we all scream for ice cream — and homemade is the very best of all. ♥

2 c. whole milk
2 c. heavy cream
1¼ c. sugar
1½ c. puréed fresh
   ripe strawberries

Bring milk & cream just to boiling point. Remove from heat, add ¾ c. of sugar, stir to dissolve. Cool. Purée the strawberries in a good processor until liquid. Add the rest of the sugar (½ c.) to purée & stir. Blend milk mixture with the purée, taste for sweetness & freeze in ice cream maker. Delicious served with a big, juicy, chocolate-dipped strawberry on top. ♥

"I wasn't kissing her, I was whispering in her mouth."

Chico Marx

50

Chocolate-Dipped Strawberries.

Sweets to the sweet — romance in berry form.

Melt really good bittersweet chocolate in a small heavy pan. Dip large (washed & dried,) perfectly ripe strawberries into the chocolate — put them on waxed paper to set. Keep refrigerated. Serve with a glass of pink champagne.

♪ "To Know, Know, Know You is to Love, Love, Love You." ♪

Phil Spector

Around the House

ROMANCE

You can set the scene for romance; a little touch here and there for the senses. Cozy up for winter, clear out clutter in spring, plant a garden.

Put out wedding pictures of family & friends & mix in a couple of those little bride & groom statues that come from tops of wedding cakes.

Decorate with large seashells in spring, a bowl of lemons or peaches in summer, baskets of apples, nuts & pears in winter.

An open cupboard with pretty china & hanging teacups is charming ~ also try hanging flowered plates on a wall.

Little dishes of candy ~ like red hots at Valentine's Day, chocolates at Christmas, candy-covered Easter eggs in spring. If you have a problem with this, get the kind you don't like!

Bouquets of romantic flowers ~ sweet peas, poppies, stock, peonies, snapdragons, freesia ~ something that smells good. Prints & paintings of fruits & flowers ~ needlepoint flower pillows; flowery anything is romantic.

Use old flowered pitchers & sugar bowls for vases.

Around the house . . .

Lace tablecloths & doilies ~ glass candlesticks in summer, wooden or brass ones in winter.

Antique linen hand towels embroidered with flowers or your initial. Dry plants in the bedrooms, teacup bouquets.

Clean up outside, sweep the porch, mow the lawn; hang a basket of flowers, put a decoration on the door, plant a sweet window box, hang a bird feeder.

I love the sound of an old ticking clock. Open windows for fresh air ~ have a fire in the winter — clean your windows & let the light in.

Hang family photos, awards, art works; a wall of foolish pictures — you & your sweetie having fun.

Flowering trees & shrubs are gorgeous. Magnolia trees look like gigantic wedding bouquets — plant lilac in purple or white, mock orange, weeping cherry trees or hydrangea.

A colorful quilt hung on a chair or over a bannister ~ a quilt holder in the bedroom.

A big fat mooshy kitty.

WHEN YOU MARRY HIM

When you marry him, love him.
After you marry him, study him.
If he is secretive, trust him.
If he is sad, cheer him.
When he is talkative, listen to him.
When he is quarrelsome, ignore him.
If he is jealous, cure him.
If he cares naught for pleasure, coax him.
If he favors society, accompany him.
When he deserves it, kiss him.
Let him think how well you understand him.
But never let him know that you manage him.

WHEN YOU MARRY HER

When you marry her, love her.
After you marry her, study her.
When she is blue, cheer her.
When she is talkative,
        by all means listen to her.
If she dresses well, compliment her.
When she is cross, humor her.
When she does you a favor, kiss her.
If she is jealous, cure her.
If she is lonely, comfort her.
When she looks pretty, tell her so.
Let her feel how well you understand her.
But never let her know she isn't boss.

TE ADORO MY LITTLE PETTY PET

" Oh Finger with the circlet slight
That keeps it warm and cosy
Wee winsome third left-handed doight
So white and warm and rosy
More taper digits there may be
More lips may kiss and cling on
This tiny finger's best to me
The one I put the ring on. "

H. Cholmondeley-Pennell

And suddenly I realised that it would all happen, I would be his wife, we would walk in the garden together, we would stroll down that path in the valley to the shingle beach. I knew how I would stand on the steps after breakfast, looking at the day, throwing crumbs to the birds, and later wander out in a shady hat with long scissors in my hand, and cut flowers for the house ♥

Daphne du Maurier

"You're all dressed up to go dreaming
Now don't tell me I'm wrong
And what a night to go dreaming
Mind if I tag along?

MOONLIGHT BECOMES YOU

Sit down and plan the trip of your life — plan it for 3 or even 5 years from now (don't worry, it will come). Choose the place of your dreams, plan where you'll stay, how you'll get there, everything about it. Dream big — half the fun IS the dream, the expectation. Now start setting a little money aside every day — & in 5 years one of the biggest dreams of your life will actually happen ♡.

We were married by the mayor of the small village where my mother lived. I wore a white dress printed with red strawberries, the children were dressed in a matching red pattern and Paolo sported a red silk tie. In all the photographs I have, we are smiling at one another, and we look happy.... For our wedding lunch we went by boat to the small island of Burano, where the famous fish restaurant 'da Romano' had prepared a glorious feast of delicacies from the lagoon.

Wind in our hair, smell of seaweed, screams of seagulls, and the island fading like a mirage in the wake of the boats....

The following day, with Paolo's daughters and my son, and a great deal of luggage, we took off from Venice airport, bound for Africa and our new life.

Kuki Gallmann

TRADITIONAL ANNIVERSARY GIFTS

1. paper, clocks
2. cotton, china
3. crystal, glass
4. fruit, flowers
5. wood, silverware
6. iron, wood
7. copper, wool
8. bronze, lace
9. pottery, leather
10. tin, aluminum
11. steel, jewelry
12. silk, linen
13. lace, textiles
14. ivory
15. crystal, timepieces
20. china, platinum
25. silver
30. pearls
35. coral, jade
40. rubies
45. sapphires
50. gold
55. emeralds
60. diamonds
75. more diamonds! ❤

FOXGLOVE

NON-TRADITIONAL
GIFTS OF LOVE

A big box of really good fireworks.

A trip to the moon on gossamer wings.

A flowering tree (an apple tree so later you can get under it as the blossoms fall – heaven!)

A star circle (planisphere) for summer nights.

A barbecue that fits in your fireplace for winter cook-ins.

Tickets: airplane, train, boat, season.

A giant bottle of champagne – 3 liters – save it for a celebration.

Feather pillows; perfume; hire someone to serenade your sweetie.

"I HAVE LEARNED THAT ONLY TWO THINGS ARE NECESSARY TO KEEP ONE'S WIFE HAPPY. FIRST, LET HER THINK SHE'S HAVING HER OWN WAY. AND SECOND, LET HER HAVE IT."
❤ LYNDON JOHNSON

wish ing on a star

"TWO SOULS BUT
WITH A SINGLE
THOUGHT—
TWO HEARTS
THAT BEAT
AS ONE."
Maria Lovell.

"WHEN TWO PEOPLE
LOVE EACH OTHER,
THEY DON'T LOOK
AT EACH OTHER,
THEY LOOK IN
THE SAME
DIRECTION."
Ginger Rogers

WE MIGHT AS WELL
FACE IT, WE'RE
ADDICTED TO LOVE."

Now in a cottage built of lilacs and laughter
I know the meaning of the words 'ever-after'.

POLKA DOTS & MOONBEAMS

" Grow old along with me
the best is yet to be... "
Robt. Browning

Some say love, it is a river
That drowns the tender reed.
Some say love, it is a razor
That leaves your soul to bleed.
Some say love, it is a hunger,
An endless aching need.
I say love, it is a flower,
And you its only seed.
It's the heart, afraid of breaking,
That never learns to dance.
It's the dream, afraid of waking,
That never takes the chance.
It's the one who won't be taken,
Who cannot seem to give —
And the soul, afraid of dying,
That never learns to live.
When the night has been too lonely,
And the road has been too long,
And you think that love is only
For the lucky and the strong —
Just remember, in the winter,
Far beneath the bitter snows —
Lies the seed, that with the sun's love
In the spring, becomes the rose.

♥Amanda McBroom

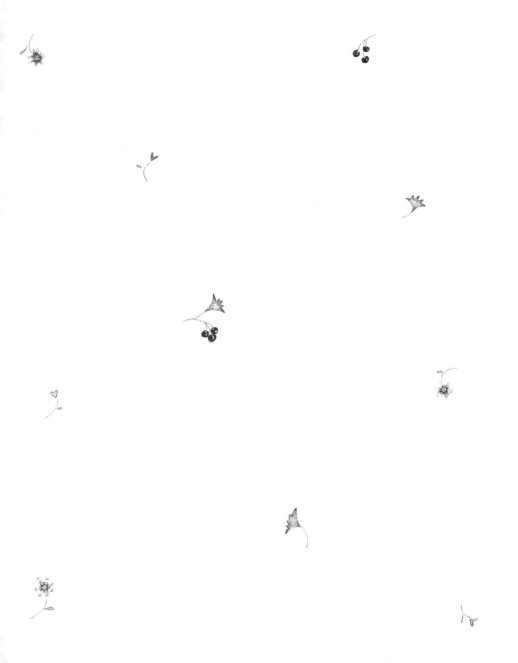